# Life's Little Lessons on

Drs Les and Leslie Parrott

eagle

Guildford, Surrey

# Introduction

No matter how some people may blanch at the idea, sooner or later everyone realizes that human beings aren't designed to 'go it alone'. If that were not the case, 'solitary confinement' might be considered some great resort activity, rather than punishment for our planet's most dastardly criminals.

Indeed, life demands that all human beings, great and small, must find their way through the maze of human relationships. Our words, attitudes and behaviours, like ripples on a pond, affect the lives of every person with whom we come in contact.

Leslie and I have made the study of relationships our life work. In so doing, we hope to gain insights for ourselves and offer help to others who are plodding along in the midst of the maze. *Life's Little Lessons on Relationships* contains the best fruit of our endeavours, as well as words of wisdom from other sources that we have gathered along the way. We hope you will find yourself strengthened as you continue your journey.

# Family

# Celebrating the Ties that Bind

In truth, most of what we think,
feel, say and do is in response
to the home
where we grew up.

The family is a classroom
where we learn the skills
that will one day enable us
to live on the outside.

Sometimes you get so far away
from your family, you think you're
outside its influence forever.
Then before you figure out
what's happening, it's right there
beside you, pulling the strings.

**Peter Collier**

When I was a boy of fourteen,
my father was so ignorant I could
hardly stand to have the old man around.
But when I got to be twenty-one,
I was astounded at how much he had learned
in seven years.

**Mark Twain**

The family you come from
isn't as important as the family
you're going to have.

**Ring Lardner**

To bring up a child in the way he should go,
travel that way yourself once in a while.

**Josh Billings**
(Henry Wheeler Shaw)

The greatest thing in family life is to
take a hint when a hint is intended
– and not to take a hint when
a hint isn't intended.

**Robert Frost**

All happy families are like one another;
each unhappy family is unhappy
in its own way.

**Leo Tolstoy**

Family is a link to our past
and a bridge to our future.

**Alex Haley**

# Relationship Booster!

At your next family gathering, make an effort to compliment each family member for at least one thing during the course of the day. Some compliments may be more challenging than others and the particularly difficult ones may require advanced planning. No matter how great the effort, the results of this exercise always exceed expectations. You will be amazed by the immediate improvement in family relations when you begin to accentuate the positive and let others know they are valued.

# Questions to Ponder

- How was love expressed in your family while you were growing up?
- How often were the words 'I love you' spoken?
- How often do you express your love for the significant people in your life?

# Questions to Ponder

• In what specific ways has your family of origin shaped your personality, your career choices, your relationships, and your values?
• Do you find it difficult to acknowledge the influence your family has had on your life and choices?

# Questions to Ponder

James 1:19 says, 'Be quick to listen and slow to speak' (NLT). That can be a tough assignment, especially with family members.

- Do you believe it is necessary to set aside time to listen to each member of your family?

- Do you often find yourself giving unsolicited advice to family members?

# **Relationship Booster!**

One of the great illusions of our age is that love is self-sustaining. It is not. Love takes time.

List the names of your immediate family members.

For one month, keep track of how much time you spend with each person on the list. You may be surprised by the results.

# Relationship *Buster*!

Families are often better at *forgiving* than *forgetting*!

Relating to family members on the basis of *who they were* rather than *who they are* will always result in disharmony.

# Friends

## Prospering in Fair Weather and Foul

This communicating of a man's self to his friend
works two contrary effects, for it redoubleth joys,
and cutteth griefs in half.

**Francis Bacon**

In prosperity our friends know us,
in adversity we know our friends.

**Churton Collins**

The only reward of virtue is virtue;
the only way to have a friend is to be one.

**Ralph Waldo Emerson**

The holy passion of friendship is
so sweet and steady and loyal and enduring
a nature that it will last through
a whole lifetime, if not asked to lend money.

**Mark Twain**

Even strong friendships require
watering, or they are sure to
shrivel up and blow away.

# Did You Know?

Friendship can help us ward off
depression, boost our immune
systems, lower our cholesterol levels,
increase our odds of surviving coronary
disease and keep stress hormones in check.

I do not believe that friends are
necessarily the people you like best,
they are merely the people
who got there first.

**Peter Ustinov**

Do not use a hatchet to remove a fly
from your friend's forehead.

**Chinese Proverb**

It takes a lot more grace to enjoy the
successes of our friends than it does
to comfort them when disaster strikes.

You can always tell a real friend; when you've made
a fool of yourself, he doesn't feel you've
done a permanent job.

**Laurence J. Peter**

Love thy neighbour as thyself, but choose
your neighbourhood.

**Louise Beal**

Genuine friendship cannot exist where
one of the parties is unwilling to hear
the truth and the other is equally
indisposed to speak it.

**Cicero**

Nothing but nothing matters more in friendship
than being true!

Woe to him who is alone when he falls
and has not another to lift him up.

**Ecclesiastes 4:10**

Friendship is like money,
easier made than kept.

**Samuel Butler**

Often we have no time for our friends but
all the time in the world for our enemies.

**Leon Uris**

When you prosper, loyal friends
applaud your successes
and cheer you on without envy.

Comfortable friends often suffer the most
from busyness and neglect.

People with deep and lasting friendships
may be introverts, extroverts, young, old, dull,
intelligent, homely, good looking;
but the one characteristic they always
have in common is openness.

**Alan Loy McGinnie**

The friends we keep the longest are often the
friends who forgave us the most.

The solid commitment between faithful friends is established by thousands of seemingly insignificant commitments over the long haul.

# Did You Know?

Having a good laugh with friends
stimulates endorphins,
the brain's natural painkillers.

Laughter is not at all a bad beginning
for a friendship, and it is far
the best ending for one.

**Oscar Wilde**

# Relationship Booster!

Alexander Graham Bell patented the telephone in 1876. Use it!

Make a list of five friends you have not spoken with in at least a year and call one, just to talk, each month for the next five months. During the sixth month, create a second list. Don't be concerned if your second list looks a lot like your first.

Word to the Wise: Don't let a misplaced telephone number stand in your way. Most people aren't in hiding and can be found easily if you are willing to make the effort.

On the road between the homes of friends,
grass does not grow.

**Norwegian Proverb**

Faithful are the wounds of a friend.

**Proverbs 27:6**

# Questions to Ponder

- What characteristics do you look for in a friend?
- Do you consider yourself a true friend?

# Relationship Booster!

How long has it been since you spoke with the people who live right next door?

It's often best to prime the pump by showing some simple gesture of kindness: shovelling the snow from your neighbour's driveway, mowing all or part of your neighbour's lawn, sharing home-baked goods, passing along fresh produce from the garden.

Use these opportunities to engage your neighbours in conversation, and watch as friendship is born.

Remember: Do more *listening* than *talking*!

# Relationship *Buster*!

B reaking a confidence is one of the easiest ways to lose a good friend.

Cover your friendships with *implied* confidentiality. That means unless you are told otherwise, conversations with good friends are 'for your ears only'.

# Romance

## Discovering the Promise of Love

Every romance runs the risk of fading.
Let me rephrase that:
Romance always fades!

Healthy, rewarding relationships are built on the following:
a strong sense of personal identity, a thriving self-esteem,
a personal sense of purpose, the ability to commit
to things outside oneself, mutual respect, good,
old-fashioned courage.

If you fail to address your hurts from
previous relationships and seek
healing, you are destined to replay
the pain again and again in
future relationships.

Immature love says,
'I love you because I need you.'
Mature love says,
'I need you because I love you.'

**Erich Fromm**

Love gives itself; it is not bought.

**Henry Wadsworth Longfellow**

The right person cannot and
will not make your life complete.
Once you have accepted that fact,
you will be eligible for a happy,
fulfilling relationship.

Once a spark of attraction catches flame,
it can quickly become a raging fire
of unreasonable passion. It's best not to
make decisions while engulfed in its heat!

Passion, though a bad regulator,
is a powerful spring.

**Ralph Waldo Emerson**

When you say, 'If this person needs me,
I'll be complete,' you are reducing others to
projects on your relationship resumé.

Love built on beauty,
soon as beauty,
dies.

**John Donne**

Passion, intimacy and commitment are
the hot, warm, and cold ingredients
in love's recipe.

Gratitude is one of the best-kept secrets
of happy dating relationships.

Dating has its own spin cycle. The excitement, anticipation, expectations, dashed hopes, demands and pressure can leave you spinning at dizzying speeds.

Commitment looks toward a future
that cannot be seen, and promises to be there.

Commitment is not as difficult as it seems,
but it does require a cool head
and a steadfast heart.

# Did You Know?

Men focus primarily on achievement and women focus primarily on relationships.

The affections are like lightning: You cannot tell
where they will strike till they have fallen.

**Jean Baptiste Lacordaire**

Infatuation has its place: But as anyone who has been in love can tell you, it's difficult to live on top of the mountain day after day.

Young love is a flame; very pretty, very hot and fierce but still only light and flickering. The love of the older and disciplined heart is as coals, deep burning, unquenchable.

**Henry Ward Beecher**

A man falls in love through his eyes,
a woman through her ears.

**Woodrow Wyatt**

Love is an act of endless forgiveness,
a tender look
which becomes a habit.

**Peter Ustinov**

Too many unsteady couples wobble to the altar –
as if getting there is the point.

What are the four most intimidating words
in a couple's vocabulary?
*'We need to talk.'*

Be forewarned: A date is often a show case,
designed to show only the best side and
conceal the shortcomings.

Some people stay in an unhappy dating relationship
because even a bad relationship can
provide a sense of security.

Love must be learned and learned
again and again;
there is no end to it.

**Katherine Anne Porter**

Love is a strange mixture of opposites:
Affection and anger, excitement and boredom,
stability and change, restriction and freedom.

Commitment creates a small
island of certainty in the swirling
waters of uncertainty.

Commitment serves as a mooring
when passion burns low
and turbulent times and fierce
impulses overtake us.

Become the kind of person
you are looking for.

People who throw kisses
are hopelessly lazy.

**Bob Hope**

Tis better to have loved and lost than
to be stuck with a real loser for
the rest of your entire,
miserable existence!

**Hallmark coffee mug slogan**

The best divorce is the one you get
*before* you get married.

**Folk saying**

Nothing takes the taste out of peanut butter
quite like unrequited love.

**Charlie Brown**

Heaven has no rage like
love to hatred turned.

**William Congreve**

Every dating relationship will include terrible,
rotten, no-good days. During these
bad times, you will learn what
your prospective mate is made of.

Instead of trying to make
someone into the ideal partner,
pour your energies into making
yourself a better person.

Some couples go into marriage thinking
they will agree on everything simply
because while they were dating, they
*seemed* to agree on everything.

Dating is tough! Trying to forge an authentic
relationship amidst all the romantic hype
is a daunting proposition.

We say 'opposites attract'
because many people are drawn to partners who
complement them – those who complete
them in some way.

For women only: You can talk to the man in
your life about your feelings, fears, and experiences,
but don't expect him to listen with the
same vigilance you would expect
from your girlfriends.

For men only: It isn't likely that the woman in your life will fully understand your 'need for space' or be willing to romanticize your independence.

If I am attached to another person because
I cannot stand on my own two feet,
he or she may be a life saver, but the
relationship is not one of love.

**Erich Fromm**

Being a woman is a terribly difficult task since it consists principally in dealing with men.

**Joseph Conrad**

Relationships are exhausting until we figure out
how to direct our energies in ways that
[the opposite gender] can truly appreciate.
Then we all win.

**John Gray**

The half life of romantic love is about three months,
after which you have only half the amount
of romantic feelings you started out with.

Some Cinderellas are longing
for a Prince Charming to come along,
turn their world inside out,
and make everything bad go away.

That's the trouble with fiction!

Men and women, women and men,
it will never work.

**Erica Jong**

## Did You Know?

The number one trait that Americans,
both men and women, claim they look
for first in a prospective mate is:
*A sense of humour!*

# Did You Know?

The number two trait that Americans, both men and women, claim to be the second thing they look for in a prospective mate is:
*Intelligence.*

It's wise to pay less attention to
your date's physical characteristics
and more attention to how he or she
responds when things go wrong.

When men and women agree,
it is only in their conclusions; their reasons
are always different.

**George Santayana**

The problem women run into when
they try to explore men's emotional
needs is that men don't want women
to explore their emotional needs!

What women want: To be loved, to be listened to,
to be desired, to be trusted, and
sometimes, just to be held.

What men want: Tickets for the world series.

**Dave Barry**

# Relationship Booster!

D o you know who you are in love with?
You may think you know. But do you really?

Many people base the quality of their romantic relationships on those things that one day will matter least. Lasting love is based on connections made deep in the heart – primarily shared values and beliefs.

When you feel yourself falling for someone, take the time to ask important questions and listen with your heart. It isn't necessary to become uncomfortably deep. Try the following:

- What is your greatest goal in life?
- If you could change the world, where would you begin?
- What is your image of the ideal family?
- What characteristic do you dislike most in a person?

# Did You Know?

Roughly half the women polled in
a recent survey said they would be
willing to cry to get their way.

Only 20 per cent of the men said they would do so.

# Did You Know?

The number one reason college students
seek counselling is for problems in
their relationships.

# Did You Know?

When asked to choose between wealth, attractiveness,
or a good personality in a relationship, the
vast majority of men and women said
they would choose a good personality.

# Questions to Ponder

An ancient Chinese proverb says, 'Patience is power. With time and patience, the mulberry leaf becomes silk.'

- How can patience increase the beauty and value of a dating relationship?

- How much time do you spend listening on a date?

# Questions to Ponder

In life, we often get what we want most!

For example, deeper and more meaningful relationships can be achieved by setting aside the fulfilment of self-centred desires.

- What do you want most?
- Are you willing to put the goals and desires of another person before your own?

# Questions to Ponder

- Why is truth so fundamental to love?
- Can love survive without truth?

# Relationship Booster!

Make a list of the characteristics you like most in the person you are dating.

You can present the list on a special occasion or simply drop them one at a time along the road to romance.

You might want to consider doing both!

When you make a habit of accentuating the positive, love almost always grows faster and stronger for both the presenter and the receiver.

# Relationship *Buster!*

Comparisons are deadly!

When you fail to appreciate the uniqueness of each person you date, you build unrealistic expectations in your own mind and insurmountable obstacles in the mind of the other person.

The past relationship whether good or bad will quickly encroach on the present.

# Marriage

## Walking in Love for a Lifetime

When the scales of a relationship are unbalanced
– one person is always giving and one is always
receiving – both will eventually feel cheated.

Spirituality is to marriage
what yeast is to bread. Ultimately, your spiritual
commitment will determine whether your
marriage rises successfully
or falls disappointingly flat.

It's no mistake that
*maturity* and *matrimony*
come from the same Latin word.

Relationships are ultimately
a deep, mysterious, and unfathomable
spiritual endeavour.

Love does not consist in
gazing at each other but in looking
together in the same direction.

**Antoine de Saint-Exupéry**

Do not let the sun go down
while you are still angry.

**Ephesians 4:26 (NIV)**

Marriage means giving up a
carefree lifestyle and coming
to terms with new limits. It means
unexpected inconveniences!

Forgiveness in marriage can only heal
when the focus is on what our spouses *do*,
rather than who they *are*.

Wise up! The little things you do now
– without thinking – will cut a life-long
groove in your relationship.

Love is like a tennis match; you'll never win
consistently until you learn to serve well.

**Dan P. Herod**

Compliments feel good –
both to give and to receive.

A happy marriage cannot survive
the cancer of resentment. Like self-pity
and blame, it eats at the human spirit
and kills the capacity for joy.

Happy couples *decide* to be happy.
In spite of the troubles life deals them,
they make happiness a habit.

The habit of happiness is an inside job.

No one can make another person unhappy.
You can't often control your circumstances,
but you can control your attitude
towards those circumstances.

Marital unhappiness is never
caused by only one person. That's why therapists
focus not on *who* is wrong, but *what* is wrong.

Living happily ever after only works if
you *make* it work.

Successful couples take the raw materials
of marriage – the good and bad they bring together
as persons – and create their
own unique and lasting bond.

The deepest kind of sharing can take place only
when there is no fear of rejection.

The more couples focus on
what they have in common,
the deeper intimacy grows.

Resentment is to relationships
as cancer is to the body. At first it is small and
imperceptible, but over time it grows larger and
spreads its poison throughout.

Faithfulness is like a multifaceted jewel,
exhibiting a complex combination of
interrelated dimensions such as trust,
commitment, truth, loyalty,
valuing and care.

Marriages can never be perfect
because people are never perfect!

What we anticipate seldom occurs;
what we least expect generally happens –
especially in marriage!

# Relationship Booster!

Praying together is a powerful
and positive element in any relationship.

In marriage, it can truly result in increased understanding
and a deeper sense of oneness.
Agree on a time to pray together for just five minutes each day.
Lay aside personal business for mutual concerns,
and each should encourage the other to pray aloud.

Love grows less exciting with time
for the same reason the second run on a fast
toboggan is less exciting than the first.

In the measure that young passion recedes,
the vacancy is replaced with a deeper, more abiding
sense of intimacy, care and co-creativity.
As the flame fades, deep-burning coals emerge.

What is the most dramatic loss
experienced in a new marriage? The idealized
image you have of your partner.

# **Did You Know?**

Every day 8 Americans over the age of 65 marry
for the first time.

# Did You Know?

A major predictor of marital satisfaction is the
husband's independence from his parents.

# Did You Know?

A survey found that 75 per cent of those polled were more tolerant of their pets' misdeeds than those of their spouses or children.

# Did You Know?

Women tend to be more distressed when their spouses
are involved with emotional infidelity.

Men are more distressed when their spouses
are involved with physical infidelity.

# Did You Know?

Relationships that lead to
marriage usually begin with the help of a third party,
such as a family member or mutual friend.

# Questions to Ponder

It is said that men 'report talk' and women 'rapport talk.'

Do you find this to be true?

151

# Questions to Ponder

When was the last time your spouse took priority over a project at work or an 'important' deadline?

# Relationship Booster!

Many people fail to express their love to the very person they love the most.

Test yourself.

Do you express your love and appreciation for your spouse:

- More than once a day?
- More than once a week?
- More than once a month?

Be honest and if you find you've been missing the boat – turn over a new leaf today!

# Relationship *Buster!*

Criticism is difficult enough, but presented in the presence of others, it can cause lasting damage to a marriage relationship.

If you must correct your spouse, do it only in the safety of your shared aloneness.

Word of Wisdom: Don't be surprised to find that the need to criticize often disappears while you're waiting for an appropriate time to address it.

# Words of Wisdom

# Walking Wisely in
# Any Relationship

Wrap and rewrap your relationships in
many layers of forgiveness.


When you talk about yourself, be willing to open up
but not too wide!

People are like tea bags, you never know how strong they are
until you see them in hot water.


Perseverance and determination are critical to relationships.
Without the ability to 'hang in there', the slightest
winds can blow a relationship off course.

You can give without loving,
but you can't love without giving.

Love seeks to *make* happy
as well as *be* happy!

Never underestimate the impact of
*one kind word!*


Being brutal and being honest
are not the same thing.

## About The Authors

**Drs Les and Leslie Parrott** are codirectors of the Center for Relationship Development on the campus of Seattle Pacific University, a groundbreaking program dedicated to teaching the basics of good relationships. Les is a professor of psychology at SPU and Leslie is a marriage and family therapist at SPU.

The Parrotts are co-authors of many books including *Becoming Soul Mates*, *The Marriage Mentor Manual*, *Questions Couples Ask*, and the award-winning *Saving Your Marriage Before It Starts*.

The Parrotts' work has been featured in such newspapers as *USA Today* and *The New York Times*. Their television appearances include CNN, *Good Morning America*, CBS *This Morning*, *World News Tonight*, and *Oprah*. The Parrotts' articles have appeared in *Christianity Today*, *Focus on the Family*, *Marriage Partnership*, *Virtue*, *Moody*, *New Man*, *Men's Health*, *Today's Christian Woman*, *Women's Day*, and many other magazines.